Missing Tiffany

Ana Benton

Published by Trellis Publishing, 2021.

MISSING TIFFANY

First edition. July 5, 2021.

Copyright © 2021 Ana Benton.

ISBN: 979-8224391721

Written by Ana Benton.

MISSING TIFFANY

ANA BENTON

The Disappearance of Tiffany Daniels

As shocking as it might seem, there are over 100,000 missing person cases active in the United States this very second. While the majority of them are eventually found, there is a large percentage of those who have been gone for years. The police extended their investigations as much as they could, and they reached the very end because there was no new information. Finally, those cases simply turn cold.

Missing person cases are particularly difficult for both families and friends. All of them are left without answers about what happened to their loved one, and they are constantly waiting for a break in the case, hoping they will have closure. The Daniels family lived through all of this in the summer of 2013 when their daughter Tiffany went missing one afternoon. It is one of the most perplexing cases in the history of Pensacola, Florida that still puzzles the investigators.

Early life

Tiffany Daniels was born on March 11th, 1988 in Dallas, Texas. She grew up in a loving and supportive family who encouraged her to follow her dreams from an early age. Tiffany loved arts, and that was evident since her high school days. She was very creative and would spend days working on a single painting. Tiffany was not shy at all and had many friends who loved spending time with her because she was always happy and positive.

After finishing high school, Tiffany felt the need to change her scenery so she moved out to Pensacola, Florida. The city had everything Tiffany craved for – long beaches, beautiful nature, and great artistic community. She was an avid hiker and loved spending time in nature. Not to forget that she often went camping on her own just to clear up her mind and relax. Tiffany loved animals, and she was a pescetarian, meaning that her diet didn't contain any meat except for the fish. She also accepted a position at Pensacola State College theater as a set designer. The pay was not spectacular, but Tiffany was doing what she loved, and she could release her artistic side.

Tiffany liked to express herself through dancing as well. It was the perfect way for her to wind down, and she would frequent blues and swing parties downtown. Everyone in those circles knew Tiffany and loved her house gatherings too. Once the dance party comes to an end, Tiffany's friends would get in their vehicles and continue having fun at her home. She was spontaneous, loved the people around her, and enjoyed life to the fullest.

Unfortunately, her caring nature got her into financial problems. Tiffany mostly lived with roommates because she was not able to cover the whole rent herself. However, those roommates would often miss their payments, and Tiffany felt bad for them. She would always pay their share even though she was struggling herself. Unfortunately, those roommates would use her kindness, and they never pay Tiffany back. In the end, Tiffany's bank account was almost empty, and she was looking for a responsible roommate who could actually afford to live with her. She ended up placing a Craigslist ad, hoping she would have more luck with the next roommate.

Gary Nichols who was 54 years old at the time saw the ad and contacted Tiffany since he needed a place to stay as soon as possible. Gary was the father of one of Tiffany's friends, and he was going through a divorce. Even though the difference in age was evident, Tiffany accepted her new roommate with open arms, and the two of them started getting along really well. Gary was financially stable, so Tiffany knew that the rent will not be a problem for him. Additionally, they had similar interests because Gary was very active, and both of them followed the same diet. Gary moved in during July of 2013, and Tiffany hoped that her issues with tenants were over.

Tiffany was in a relationship at the time, and her boyfriend's name was Grey Thomas. They met in the summer of 2012 at a dance party and were inseparable since then. He just got accepted to the graduate program at the University of Texas located in Austin. He decided to move there and urged Tiffany to join him. However, Tiffany was not eager to leave Florida, but she still wanted to have a long-distance relationship with him. The two have made plans for her to visit in a couple of weeks, and Tiffany was happy because it was clear he cared about her as well. Grey hoped Tiffany will like Austin and that she would eventually change her mind about moving there.

The day of the disappearance

Tiffany's boyfriend was supposed to head out to Texas on August 11th, 2013 and the two of them met for a breakfast where they said goodbyes to each other. They will be apart for a couple of weeks and simply had to spend some time together before his trip. Gary Nichols saw Tiffany that afternoon, and he did notice that she was a bit sad about the fact that her boyfriend was leaving which was understandable. But she soon started talking about the trip to Austin she was planning and her mood brightened up immediately.

Since Pensacola State College theater was preparing to start the production of the musical called *Spamalot*, Tiffany had a lot of work ahead of her. *Spamalot* was based on the movie called *Monty Python and the Holy Grail* so Tiffany decided to re-watch it just to get inspired. After all, she was in charge of the set and wanted to do a great job. Gary Nichols was at the house, so he joined her in front of the TV set. The two watched the movie up until midnight and then went to sleep. Both of them had to get up early for work. Sometime around 05:00 AM Gary heard the front door opening and closing several times. He thought it must be Tiffany, but he was a bit confused because he knew that she was not an early riser. As a matter of fact, her job started at 08:00 AM so this was very unusual.

Gary got up and went work at 07:00 AM. The first thing he noticed when he exited the house was that Tiffany's car was gone. He assumed she went to work earlier because it was the first day of *Spamalot* production. Tiffany probably wanted to get more things done. Tiffany's boss did confirm that she showed up for work on schedule but asked him to leave earlier. Tiffany also mentioned that she will not be in town for a couple of days and wanted to inform him about it. Tiffany didn't mention where she was going and didn't provide any additional information. The boss simply concluded that she might have some family business, or wanted to go camping. Tiffany left the theater around 04:45 PM.

Gary came home from work as usual but Tiffany wasn't there. It was strange because she didn't mention she was leaving or anything similar. Tiffany was very responsible and would always tell her friends and family about her plans. Even though Gary was her roommate for a short time, he got to know Tiffany and was sure that she would bring up an upcoming trip. Gary called his daughter Noel who was Tiffany's friend and asked her if she knew anything about Tiffany's whereabouts. She told him not to worry and that Tiffany would show up soon because she was probably staying with friends or working overtime.

The power was cut off the next day, and Gary assumed that Tiffany forgot to pay the bills. He tried contacting her, but nobody answered the cell phone. Worried that something happened to her, he once again urged his daughter Noel to contact Tiffany's mother Cindy and see if she could get a hold of her. Noel sent her a Facebook message, and Tiffany's mother brushed it off because her daughter was a free spirit and had a tendency to go out in nature. Perhaps she had no signal, or she didn't hear the phone ringing. But as the days went on without a single word from Tiffany, everyone started feeling a bit uneasy about the situation.

The search for Tiffany

Tiffany's family got really concerned after they realized that they couldn't reach her for several days. Her cell phone kept ringing, but nobody was answering. Cindy Daniels decided to start calling Tiffany's friends to see if anyone knew where her daughter was. She contacted Noel Nichols, and the two of them made a list of people they should contact. As they went through the list, they realized that no one had seen Tiffany for a week and they all assumed she was staying with another friend. Cindy was really worried, and she contacted the law enforcement to report that her daughter was missing.

Cindy went straight to Escambia County sheriff's office, but the law enforcement didn't take her seriously. They did send out a patrol car to her house to take a statement. The officers thought that since Tiffany was young and free-spirited, she is probably somewhere having a blast and she would turn up soon. But Cindy persisted, and they took a closer look at the case. Escambia County sheriff's office realized that the missing person case was not in their jurisdiction because Tiffany lived in Pensacola and that was also the location she was last seen at. Pensacola Police Department was not dismissive of the report, and they were quickly out on the scene.

Cindy was already at Tiffany's place of residence when the detective Daniel Harnett arrived there to investigate if there was anything suspicious in the house. Tiffany's mother was asked to wait in front of the house. The detective and an officer went through the rooms together and found Tiffany's camping gear. This meant that she wasn't taking a break somewhere in the woods. There were also no signs that she packed her things for any type of trip. Detective Harnett asked Cindy about Tiffany's personal life, focusing on her boyfriend Grey Thomas. Cindy told him that he left for Texas one day before Tiffany's disappearance and this made Detective Harnett focus on the possibility that Tiffany decided to follow him there. However, one of Tiffany's closest friends said: *"Tiffany was a very spontaneous person, but she was also a reliable person. My opinion is if she said that she would be somewhere, she would be there."*

Rodney Daniels, Tiffany's father called Grey Thomas to see if she was there with him. He told him that he spoke to Tiffany on the day of his arrival to Texas, but he hasn't heard from her afterward. Knowing that the majority of disappearances are often followed by a murder, Detective Harnett couldn't rule out the option that Grey returned to Pensacola one day later and hurt Tiffany for some reason. He contacted Grey, asking him to go to his local police station and give them his DNA. They needed to have it in a database in case some new evidence turns up during the investigation. Curious about Grey's whereabouts on the day of the disappearance, Detective Harnett requested Grey's cellphone data. It showed that Grey was in Austin, Texas since the day he left Pensacola.

Running out of reasons for the disappearance, the investigators started interviewing the entire family. They started viewing the case as a possible suicide, so Detective Harnett asked a lot of questions about Tiffany's mental state. Her sister Candace McAdams who lived out of state was very close to Tiffany. The two of them spoke over the phone at least a couple of times every week. Candace mentioned that she noticed a change in Tiffany's behavior sometime in 2012. She was not as happy as she used to be and Candace though that she might be keeping something from her. But nobody could be certain that she was depressed or had any mental problems.

After questioning the neighbors, the investigators found out that Tiffany did come back home after work on the day of her disappearance. Her car was seen briefly in front of the house. Gary Nichols was there at the time, but he didn't see her come in. He was talking with his girlfriend on the phone, and the chances are he was simply too engaged in the conversation to register that someone opened the front door. Cindy thought this was strange because the house itself wasn't large. She stated: *"In Tiffany's room the top of her closet had a foot missing of it. Clear through to the next room. You could throw something through it. I find it hard to believe he couldn't hear her through the room but he heard her going in and out of the house early in the morning.*" However, the police dismissed Gary as a suspect because there were no traces of foul play anywhere, and he was the first one to start worrying about Tiffany. Detective Hartnett said: "*Gary seemed appropriate. There was nothing unclear in anything he told us to raise an alarm.*"

The discovery of the car

Detective Harnett alerted the media right away about Tiffany's 1999 Toyota 4Runner car, hoping that someone might have seen it somewhere. The TV stations broadcasted the images for days, while Tiffany's friends went around Pensacola, putting up the fliers. And soon enough, the police had their first solid lead. Tiffany's car was spotted at a parking lot at Park West in Pensacola Beach. A jogger who was out running on the morning of August 20th, 2013 thought that the vehicle looked familiar and connected the dots. He also knew the Daniels family, as well as Tiffany herself. Tiffany's mother said: "*I felt something bad happened as soon as they located the car. I believed she was still on the island and that we would find her.*"

Once the police arrived, they inspected the abandoned car. It was not too dirty from the outside, and it looked like it was out in the elements for a couple of days. They found Tiffany's bicycle on the inside, alongside her purse, a wallet, a cell phone, a couple of paintings, a jar of peanut butter, and a bottle of water. The forensic team analyzed the car and found two suspicious fingerprints on the car and the steering wheel. After a thorough examination, they determined that the fingerprints didn't belong to Tiffany or any of the officers who were on the scene. Then they proceeded to run them through the database but got no hits.

The parking lot where the car was found was right next to the beach. It was a very popular spot for both locals and tourists. Tiffany's friends and family though that someone must have seen something in the days following the disappearance. The police weren't enthusiastic about it because Tiffany's car was not very distinctive and they were certain nobody would have noticed when it arrived or who was driving it. Not to forget that there were two condominium complexes on the other side of the parking lot. It was summertime and people would usually hang out on their balconies, trying to cool down from the heat.

Tiffany's friends started going around, handing out the flyers, and talking to the people living in the apartment buildings. One resident told them that he was sure the car was not in the parking lot two days ago because he has a good view of it and would have noted if a particular vehicle was parked there for a longer period of time. A couple of people said that they saw a man driving and exiting the car. All of the information was written down and presented to the detectives. They were conducting their own investigation at the time that included toll booths at the Bob Sikes Bridge.

Since Park West was located on Santa Rosa Island, only one bridge connected it to the mainland. The bridge has toll booths, and every vehicle that crosses over is captured by the surveillance cameras. Unfortunately, the cameras monitor the license plates only so finding out who was driving the car was impossible. On the other hand, this information would provide the investigators with the exact time when Tiffany's Toyota crossed the bridge. The detectives went through the images of vehicles that entered Santa Rosa Island on the day Tiffany disappeared and discovered that her car passed the toll booths on August 12th, 2013 at 07:51 PM. This was three hours after she left the theater.

The search of Santa Rosa Island

The detectives, as well as the family, had many theories about what might have happened to Tiffany on Santa Rosa Island. The forensic team determined that the tires of her bike had sand on them which led them to speculate that she went on a ride that night. She might have placed the bike in her car and proceeded to the beach to watch the meteor shower or take a swim in the ocean. The currents are incredibly strong in that area, and she could have been pulled under, unable to swim back to the shore.

Led by this thought, the detectives suspected that her body might appear on the shore of Santa Rosa Island. The island itself was large and searching it would be quite a task. Tiffany's parents found out about KLAAS organization that would gather up the volunteers from the area in order to search for missing children. They contacted the people in charge, and they agreed to help out with the search of Santa Rosa Island. The teams had a lot of grounds to cover, but they had plenty of help from the other search organizations in Florida. They searched the island by foot, going through the entire national park. There was no sign of Tiffany or any items that could be connected to her.

The fact that they didn't find any traces was encouraging to Tiffany's family because this meant that she might be alive somewhere. But it was unlikely that she was still on the island. They needed to widen up the search and let everyone know that Tiffany was missing. Noel Nichols decided to set up a Facebook page in order to help find Tiffany. She uploaded her photos as well as the images of her distinctive foot tattoos. Other users were sharing the information, and soon the tips started coming in.

The sightings

Noel sent every single information she got through the Facebook page to the detective working on this case. Detective Daniel Harnett, eager to find Tiffany, was willing to check every possible sighting. A few weeks after setting up the page, Noel received a tip from a local store. A clerk claimed that Tiffany entered the shop and bought some groceries. He was able to provide a full description of the girl which sparked the interest. Unfortunately, Detective Harnett asked for the surveillance tapes, and Tiffany was not on them. The clerk simply wanted to become a part of the investigation at any cost.

But the next possible sighting gave Tiffany's parents hope that she was out there somewhere. A waitress from Metairie, Louisiana sent a message through Facebook in January of 2014 saying that she might have seen Tiffany a couple of weeks after her disappearance. The woman didn't contact anyone because she was not sure if the girl in the restaurant was indeed Tiffany. However, she couldn't stop thinking about it and decided to let the family know. There was something strange about that encounter, and the waitress thought that it might be important.

She recalls that three women came into the restaurant one night. Two of them were younger, while the third one was significantly older than them. The older woman wore expensive clothes, while the other two did not. They also had long sleeved shirts, which was an odd sight in New Orleans during the summer and autumn. The waitress found it unusual that the older woman was the only one communicating with her. The young women simply sat there in silence, trying not to make an eye contact with the waitress. One of them spoke up to ask if the soups on the menu had fish in them, and the waitress took a good look at her face. It seemed familiar to her and she asked right away if she was the woman who went missing in Florida.

The mood at the table shifted instantly. The whole group got up and left the restaurant. The tip sounded credible because Tiffany was a pescetarian, and she was very concerned about her diet. The family asked if the waitress could provide any surveillance videos that would give them proof that Tiffany was there. She told them that the tapes were long gone because they record over the old footage regularly. While this didn't give the investigators any concrete proof that Tiffany was out there, the tip led Tiffany's family to form another theory – that she was a victim of human trafficking.

White Tiffany didn't fit the profile of a typical human trafficking victim, nothing can be dismissed in this case. There was a possibility that she was kidnapped from the beach and transported to New Orleans soon after her disappearance. Tiffany's family dug deeper and found connections with another incident when a young woman was taken to the same city by two men. She was then forced to become a sex worker. Human trafficking is an ongoing problem in the United States, and the police are doing everything in order to prevent it.

However, they simply cannot save all of the victims right away. Instead, they are familiar with the known human trafficking routes and the local patrol cars often monitor the movement on them. One of the routes is the Interstate 10 that passes through Pensacola. This very fact made Tiffany's parents believe that she met someone on the night of the disappearance and they probably took advantage of her. Tiffany was friendly and loved talking to other people. She might have bumped into someone who seemed trusting but had bad intentions. Unfortunately, the police still had little information, and they were unable to pursue this tip. The case remained open, but there were no new leads.

The revival of the case

The Investigation Discovery channel was aware of the case, and they decided to include it in the new season of their popular show called *Disappeared*. In it, they cover the missing person cases hoping that the media exposure would prompt the possible witnesses to contact the authorities and provide them with new details that could revive the case. Their crew visited Pensacola and talked to almost everyone involved with the investigation, including the lead detective and Tiffany's parents. The whole city knew that the Investigation Discovery crew was there and people were once again talking about the case.

Four months after they completed the filming, Pensacola Police Department was contacted by a new eyewitness who claimed they had information about the case. The witness told Detective Hartnett that they saw a man opening the trunk of Tiffany's car on the parking lot in Park West. The man was wearing red shorts, and he was in his thirties. This confirmed the statements made by the tenants from the nearby apartment building who claimed that the vehicle was driven by a man. Unfortunately, they weren't able to identify the said individual.

Tiffany Daniels' disappearance is still being investigated, and the authorities are hoping that someone will come forward soon. There has not been a confirmed sighting since August 12th, 2013 but they are not ruling out the possibility that she is alive. The investigators never found her body, so any scenario is possible. The family and friends are managing the Facebook page about Tiffany, and they are updating it regularly, doing their best to keep her in the media. The case remains a true mystery that will hopefully be resolved one day.

THE DISAPPEARANCE OF KELSIE SCHELLING

ANA BENSON

Every time a woman goes missing or is found murdered, the police usually takes a closer look at their spouses or boyfriends. It is a standard procedure, especially if there were indications that they were in a troubled relationship. The disappearance of Kelsie Schelling is one of the biggest mysteries in Colorado. This young pregnant woman was last seen in February of 2013 and the case is still open to this day.

However, Kelsie's family was quite disappointed at the lack of interest by the police to investigate her then-boyfriend Donthe Lucas, who was clearly involved in this crime. After all, Donthe did invite Kelsie to his hometown on that fateful night and he was the last person who saw her alive. When they realized that the police are stalling with the investigation, the family made a promise that Kelsie's case will not be forgotten until they discover what really happened. They kept the public informed through their Facebook page and eventually managed to reach the Colorado Bureau of Investigation.

Early life

Kelsie Jean Schelling was born on 18th February 1991 in Holyoke, Colorado. She grew up in a tightknit family and later became even closer to her mother after the divorce of her parents. Kelsie was only eleven years old when they split up but she would often talk to her father as well. However, they didn't see each other that often because he moved to a different part of town. After graduating from high school, Kelsie attended Northeastern Junior College located in Sterling, Colorado. She was fascinated with psychology and planned to major in it once she gets accepted to the university.

Kelsie was friendly and outspoken, so it comes as no surprise that she had many friends and was a life of every party. During her time at Northeastern Junior College, Kelsie met Donthe Lucas. He was a star player on the basketball team and the two of them fell in love instantly. Donthe Lucas had a very difficult childhood and he grew up in Pueblo, Colorado which is an infamous place known for higher crime rates than anywhere else in the state. He loved basketball and it was clear that he would be an outstanding athlete even in high school. Basketball players do have enormous salaries so Donthe Lucas did see it as an opportunity to help his family out further down the line.

He was hoping that a scout would attend one of his games and recruit him for one of bigger colleges or universities that had a good basketball team. But his big break never happened. Instead, he ended up in Northeastern Junior College which was alright, but Donthe wasn't quite happy with that outcome. His dissatisfaction was evident even in the relationship with Kelsie. Their romance had constant ups and downs, and the two of them would break up, and get back together which drove Kelsie mad. They did finally call it quits after several semesters, and didn't see each other for quite some time.

After finishing the two years at the junior college, Kelsie pursued her education even further, and she moved to California to attend Vanguard University in Costa Mesa. She was finally able to study psychology full time. Donthe continued to play basketball for Emporia State University in Kansas. Kelsie's family was happy she managed to end her relationship with the troubled basketball player, and they hoped that she would make a new life far away from Colorado. Kelsie was independent and she enjoyed living and studying in California. When she wasn't attending classes, Kelsie worked at a tanning salon with her best friend. However, she did drop out of the college because the school work was a bit too much for her at the time and her only option was to go back home. She moved to Denver in 2012 and started working in a store. Meanwhile, Donthe Lucas was back in his hometown Pueblo.

The two of them started talking once again during the autumn of 2012. It was obvious that they still had feelings for each other, so no one was surprised when Donthe and Kelsie decided to spend the Christmas holidays together. The couple seemed happy to everyone around them, but Kelsie did tell her friends that their relationship was still very toxic. Donthe was still treating her badly, calling her names, and starting unnecessary fights. Soon enough everything will change. A few weeks after the holidays, Kelsie found out that she was pregnant. Shocked at first, Kelsie was lost and decided not to tell anyone for a couple of weeks. But keeping a secret was hard. So she called her mother and told her the news. Kelsie's mother Laura would later say that even though her daughter felt a bit stressed, she was still excited about the pregnancy. Yes, she was young but Kelsie was determined to make it work.

Donthe Lucas didn't take the news so well. Having in mind how dissatisfied he felt about his failed basketball career, it is not wrong to assume that the news about a baby simply solidified the fact that his dreams will never come true. Kelsie noticed the change in his mood and openly told him that he doesn't have to be a part of their baby's life. But it is also worth mentioning that Kelsie confided in her best friend that Donthe was ecstatic to become a father at one point. However, his mind was constantly changing. Kelsie went to see her doctor on 4th of February 2013 and he confirmed that she was eight weeks pregnant. The baby was healthy and doing well. The doctor provided her with an ultrasound of the unborn baby, and she was full of joy. Kelsie immediately sent out the pictures to her mother, her friends, and Donthe. Unfortunately, the excitement will not last forever.

The night of the disappearance

Donthe and Kelsey exchanged several emails on February 3rd, 2013. He invited her to visit him in Pueblo. She turned him down saying that she needs to go for a checkup the next day to make sure everything is alright with the baby. After seeing her doctor on the morning of February 4th, 2013, Kelsie went straight to the store. She worked the second shift and was expected to come home sometime after 10:00 PM that night. However, she was in contact with Donthe for the entire day, texting back and forth about the pregnancy. Donthe told her that she should drive out to Pueblo after work because he had a surprise for her. Not knowing what it is, Kelsie asked for more information because Pueblo is two hours away from Denver, and she would probably be tired after work. He insisted that she would be happy with his surprise and that he cannot tell her anything over the phone.

It is safe to assume that Kelsie thought that Donthe was ready to change and start a family with her. Their relationship wasn't a standard one but it seemed like Kelsie was willing to move past all the negative things and focus on the future. So after her shift ended, Kelsie got in her Chevy Cruze LTZ and drove to Pueblo in the middle of the night. Donthe was supposed to meet her in a parking lot in front of a local Walmart. The surveillance cameras did confirm that Kelsie got there on time, but Donthe was nowhere to be seen. She waited in a parked car for almost an hour before sending another text message to Donthe, saying that she has been in the parking lot for too long and that she would come pick him up at whatever location he is at the moment. She got a reply sometime around 12:15 AM.

Donthe told her that he will be waiting for her in the street next to his grandmother's home. Kelsie is seen exiting the parking lot a couple of minutes after she got the message. She clearly did arrive at the second rendezvous spot, but once again Donthe wasn't there. Kelsie sent him another message asking where is he and Donthe replied that he will be there in a minute. This is the last known communication between these two until sometime before 04:00 AM. After going through the phone records, police did discover that Donthe called Kelsie at 03:54 AM but she didn't pick up. The significance of this mysterious phone call will be revealed later. After reviewing the cell tower pings for both phones, the investigators did discover that they were in close proximity to each other.

The search for Kelsie

Kelsie's mother Laura got really worried the next day because she wasn't able to reach her daughter over the phone. She tried calling numerous times but it went straight to the voicemail. The last message she got from her daughter was the ultrasound image of her unborn child, and Laura wasn't sure if something happened to Kelsie after work, or she was ignoring her calls. Laura contacted Kelsie's friends who told her that she went to Pueblo to meet with Donthe. With no word from her daughter, she called Donthe who picked up his phone and told Laura that he had seen Kelsie last night, but that she drove back home in the morning.

Laura was starting to panic, but she did tell Donthe that she would involve the police if she doesn't hear from her daughter soon. Laura and Kelsie were very close and they did tell each other everything, but she suspected that her daughter kept this information from her because she didn't want Laura to know that she was meeting with Donthe. After all, Laura was aware of the nature of their relationship, and his reluctance to accept the baby. Plus, Laura would probably advise Kelsie not to go to Pueblo in the middle of the night.

Laura contacted the local law enforcement and told them that her daughter was missing. Without any solid leads or evidence, they started asking around for Kelsie. Their first step was to take a closer look at Donthe because he claimed that he was the last person to saw Kelsie. She did travel from Denver just to see him. After checking Kelsie's credit card records, they did notice that the card was used hours after Kelsie's last known contact with Donthe. They reviewed the surveillance of the ATM and noticed that Donthe had the card and picked up $400 from Kelsie's account. They weren't sure if Donthe had Kelsie's agreement to use the card, but that was a felony in the state of Colorado, so he was led to the police station for questioning. He had a lot of things to clear up, starting with the timeline of Kelsie's visit to Pueblo.

Donthe's interview

After being picked up by the police, Donthe told his own version of the story. They did see each other that night and talked until early morning hours. Donthe and Kelsie got into a fight and she felt too agitated to drive back home to Denver. She was also very tired from working the second shift. Instead, Kelsie decided to sleep in her car which was parked near his grandmother's house. According to Donthe, his phone rang sometime around 07:00 AM and it was Kelsie. She wasn't feeling well and asked Donthe to drive her to a hospital. He put on his clothes, got to her car, and drove her to the Parkview Hospital.

Kelsie wasn't sure if something happened to the baby during their argument last night and she insisted to see a doctor before she heads out to Denver. Donthe sat inside her car in the parking lot for two hours when she finally emerged from the hospital. Kelsie told him that she had lost the baby. She then asked Donthe to drive her to Walmart to get something to eat and buy some snacks for the road. The two of them started fighting while they were in Walmart and Kelsie refused to drive him home. Donthe simply walked away and got to his grandmother's house on foot. He didn't see Kelsie later in the day and he assumed she went home. He didn't mention stopping at the ATM to pick up the money during his initial interview.

The investigators did notice a couple of possible leads that could collaborate Donthe's story, namely the Parkview Hospital. Each medical facility keeps detailed records of the patients they treat. After speaking to the staff and going through the data, they have confirmed that Kelsie didn't check in during the morning of February 5th. There were also numerous surveillance cameras all over the building and none of them picked up Kelsie entering or leaving the hospital. It was obvious that this part of Donthe's story was not true.

Of course, the police investigators decided to check out Walmart as well because the parking lot and stores do have surveillance cameras, and they might have picked up something that would be of use. While they couldn't find Kelsie or Donthe entering the Walmart, they did notice Kelsie's car on the parking lot. However, the timeline didn't match up with Donthe's story because Kelsie's car appeared at noon, and not in the morning. Plus, Donthe was the only passenger in the car. Another surveillance camera which was positioned on the back side of Walmart did record Donthe getting into his mother's car – another detail he failed to mention in the initial talk with the investigators.

Without any proof that Donthe's version of the events is true, they called him up for a second interview. The investigators did have a plan this time - they wanted to find out more about the ATM, and how it fits into his timeline. He told the detectives that he took $400 in order to pay his bills and that Kelsie lent him the money since he was at the ATM while Kelsie was at the hospital. When the detectives told Donthe that there is no record of Kelsie ever being in that hospital, his reply was: "I don't even know what to say right now."

They also presented him with Walmart surveillance video that proves Donthe was the only person in the car. He was surprised with the evidence put in front of him, and before the detectives managed to get him to open up, he decided to lawyer up. He was only charged with the identity theft due to the fact that he used Kelsie's credit card, but the case was dropped. The judge had determined that Donthe did use Kelsie's credit card in the past and it was a normal behavior. However, nobody managed to figure out why Donthe had her card in the first place. After all, if Kelsie decided to ran away and start a new life, she would need the money, as well as her vehicle.

Speaking of Kelsie's car, the investigators took a closer look at the surveillance video from Walmart parking lot because they wanted to follow the vehicle. Exactly one day after Donthe left Kelsie's car there, another man approached the car and got inside by using the key. He didn't break in or steal the car. The man was dressed in black, wearing a hoodie, so identifying him was almost impossible. His body type was different than Donthe's, and the mystery man was significantly shorter. Keep in mind that Donthe was a tall basketball player, so his height would be noticeable, even in a low-quality video.

Seeing the direction in which the car went, the police collected the surveillance videos from stores and businesses which were in close proximity. They put the puzzle pieces together and found a route but they couldn't follow it all the way. One day later, the car was dropped at the parking lot of Saint Mary Corwin Hospital. The man locked the car and walked away. The investigators located the vehicle on 14th of February, 2013 and figured out the timeline. But nobody knows where the car was during 6th of February. There weren't any signs of a struggle that would indicate that Kelsie was killed in her car. Almost all of her personal items were missing, including her wallet and a backpack.

While it is unclear if the vehicle was tested for the traces of DNA, an unnamed police officer who worked for Pueblo Police Department will later say that they did find bodily fluids in the trunk of Kelsie's car, as well as two palm prints. However, no one knows what happened with this evidence and was it ever tested. It is simply another thing which the police investigators decided to ignore in this case. Unfortunately, the whole investigation will be under scrutiny soon after.

Theories

Figuring out a solid theory without too many evidence or information can be challenging. Laura, Kelsie's mother, claims that her daughter was probably murdered and that it was premeditated. The first red flag for her was Donthe's initial invitation to meet him before the doctor's appointment. When Kelsie refused, he knew that he had to act fast. Donthe lured Kelsie to Pueblo by saying that he has something to show her, but he never gave an explanation to the law enforcement about what the surprise really was.

It is clear that Kelsie was alive and well up until the point she met Donthe in the street next to his grandmother's house. This is where the trail goes cold. The activity on her phone stops until 04:00 AM. If we analyze the location of the phones, another theory is that Donthe led Kelsie to a remote location and harmed her. It was possible that Kelsie dropped her phone in the middle of a struggle. Donthe couldn't find the phone in the dark, so he had to call her number. He was very likely getting rid of the evidence.

There is a possibility that the two of them did indeed get into a fight, and that an unfortunate accident happened. However, it is more likely that Donthe planned to get rid of Kelsie, and had planned every single step he would take that night. He really insisted to see her as soon as possible. While it is not fair to put the blame on the rest of Lucas family, the fact that his mother picked him up immediately after he left Kelsie's vehicle at the Walmart's parking lot indicates that she knew what was going on. Pueblo Police Department did stop investigating Donthe, and they claimed they didn't have enough physical evidence to prove that a crime really occurred. But they did receive a couple of noteworthy tips which were ignored and never pursued.

The missed opportunities

The entire investigation of the disappearance of Kelsie Schelling was troubling from the very beginning. While the detectives did not have physical evidence of a crime, it was clear that Donthe was the last person who saw Kelsie alive. In every standard investigation, he would have been the prime suspect, and the investigators would do their best to find more proof that he was somehow connected to the crime. The cell tower pings did show that both of their phones were in a remote area next to Pueblo in the early morning hours.

But there are even bigger missed opportunities that could have provided the investigators with the proof they needed. For instance, Donthe was living in his grandmother's house at the time of Kelsie's disappearance. However, the entire family moved out soon after. The landlord started redecorating the house because he wanted to rent it again. He did hear about the missing girl from Denver but had no idea about the details of the case, or the fact that the Lucas family was involved in any way.

He decided to put the new carpets in and when he lifted the old one, the landlord noticed a strange stain on the bottom. He contacted the police enforcement because he was worried that something bad has happened in the house. However, the police ignored his request to check out the stained carpet, and no one had ever arrived at Lucas' previous residence to pick it up. The landlord ended up throwing the carpet away because he simply couldn't keep it forever in the house and wanted to move on with the renovation.

Another missed opportunity involved a couple of fishermen who were out on a lake on a night fishing expedition. It is important to mention that the lake was located near the Saint Mary Corwin Hospital. As you might recall, that was the spot where the police officers discovered Kelsie's vehicle on the 14th of February 2013. They were out on a bank when a hook got stuck to something poking out of the sand. The fishermen went to investigate and were sure that they saw a part of a human ribcage, as well as a skull.

They were terrified by that discovery and left the area right away. Both of them were reluctant to notify the police because they did have some troubles with the law in the past. But that didn't stop them from telling this story to their friends who urged them to contact the local law enforcement. A couple of months passed before they finally talked to the police, but the lake wasn't searched afterward.

The current searches

Family and friends continued to search for Kelsie even after it was clear that the police enforcement forgot about her case. They created a Facebook group that was constantly updated with new information. Pueblo Police Department did go through many changes after Kelsie went missing. The lead investigator was replaced with a new one who was willing to cooperate with the Schelling family. The Schellings did offer a large reward for any new leads that might help them locate their missing daughter. The reward was $100,000 at one point.

This eventually led to false claims and misleading messages such as the one which claimed that Kelsie was still alive, but was placed into a sex traffic ring after a hired hitman decided not to kill her. Laura Schelling contacted the police and told them about the message. Since the investigators decided to follow every lead possible, they dug deeper and even involved the FBI. Their experts did manage to trace the message back to Russia through the IP address so it was clear that this tip was useless.

The biggest break in the case happened in the spring of 2017 when Colorado Bureau of Investigation finally got the authorization from the local law enforcement to join the search. CBI did determine that the prime suspect should be Donthe Lucas, and they got the warrant to search the area around his previous place of residence. A large number of police officers was seen around that house during April of 2017, and they dug up the parts of the backyard using heavy machinery.

The search has been successful and the officers left the scene carrying bags of evidence. However, they stated that they didn't find any traces of Kelsie's remains. Kelsie's family released the following statement after the search: "The past 2 days have been grueling and emotional, ending with the outcome we did not hope for. Kelsie is still missing. There is no way for me to convey to you all the pain that I feel right now. Sincere, heartfelt thanks goes out to the members of Pueblo PD, CBI and Parks & Rec who worked so hard on this search for Kelsie. This was a physically demanding excavation for them and we witnessed how hard they worked. Despite all the issues we have had in the past, the new leadership over Kelsie's case from PPD and active involvement from CBI is giving us hope that an effective investigation is finally taking place."

The case is still active and the police didn't arrest Donthe. But the positive changes are happening and Kelsie's family is certain that they will find the answers they are looking for now that the investigation is finally moving forward.

FOREVER MISSING: THE DISAPPEARANCE OF NATALEE HOLLOWAY

NATHAN NIXON

Natalee Holloway Disappearance

The tragic story of Natalee Holloway still remains a mystery to this day. The events prior to her disappearance are centered on unreliable witnesses, investigators not following proper procedures, and friends who had left her alone with local patrons. To say that a school trip is never supposed to turn out this way is a monumental understatement. Several theories exist as to what really happened to Natalee. The one, glaring truth of the matter is that Natalee was a beautiful, vibrant young woman who is gone far too soon. Many other facts exist. Witnesses, however, do not.

Natalee Holloway was born in 1986 to David and Elizabeth Holloway in Clinton, Mississippi. Following her parents mutual divorce in 1993, she was raised by her mother alongside her younger brother. Natalee made her life in Alabama when her mother re-married to George Twitty. It was here that she prospered in many organizations, extracurricular activities, and academic niches. Natalee attended Mountain Brook High School in Mountain Brook, Alabama. She was a prominent member in the National Honor Society, was a leader on the school dance team, and competed several sports. Through her hard work, she had earned a full scholarship to attend the University of Alabama, where she enter a pre-med course track and eventually earn her Doctorate. This was all assuming she would make it to the next fall.

Upon graduation, 124 graduating Mountain Brook High School seniors took an "unofficial" school trip to Aruba. Aruba is a Dutch holding in the Caribbean. The group of students arrived in Aruba on May 26, 2005. The trip was scheduled for five days. Oddities of this trip were already apparent. While the trip had 7 chaperones, the students were not expected to be watched every second. The chaperones would meet with the full group of students each night to make sure that everything was okay. To say that these students were taking advantage of this was an understatement. "There was wild partying, lots of drinking, lots of room switching every night," Police Commissioner Gerold Dompig, who headed the investigation from mid-2005 to late 2016, said. "We are aware that the Holiday Inn told them they were absolutely not welcome back next year. Natalee, we know, drank all day every day while there. We have statements that proclaim she started every morning with cocktails. Often times so much drinking that she didn't show up for breakfast on two separate mornings."

Liz Cain and Claire Foreman, two of Holloway's classmates, agreed. "The drinking was excessive. We all were going too far and didn't understand the dangers"

Jodi Bearman organized the class trip. The investigation that would soon follow turned up numerous mistakes and irresponsibility's on the part of organizers and chaperones. The obvious problem was the supervision. How can seven chaperones have control of 124 high school graduates in a foreign place? These students were essentially given the freedom to do whatever they wanted with no punishment. Investigators and parents alike could not believe the lack of supervision and authority displayed by the adults. The punishment that Natalee Holloway would suffer was far greater than anyone could have imagined. However, the fact that this was an avoidable mistake is obvious. Natalee Holloway should never have been allowed to be in this position.

It was May 29, 2005. Natalee had packed her luggage and prepared all of her things to board the flight home the next morning. She had positioned her luggage neatly at the foot of her bed and cleaned up her hotel room accordingly. The 124 graduates had one last night of fun before it was time to head home. This was the last time she would be in her hotel room.

Natalee went out on the town with several of her classmates on night of May 29. Typical of the previous nights, she and her classmates had been heavily drinking and interacting with numerous locals. Natalee had a contagious personality and could always strike up a conversation with anyone. As the night drew on into morning, they arrived at Carlos'n Charlies. This was a well-known bar and dance club in the heart of Aruba. Natalee would last be seen at approximately 1:30 A.M. on May 30, 2005. The story was only just beginning.

Natalee had met up with locals seemingly every night she went out. Striking up conversations, drinking excessively, and trusting strangers was common by several of the graduates that were there. The last glimpse of Natalee would prove to be the beginning of a complicated, international investigation that would prove nearly impossible to solve. She left the club that morning with 17-year-old Joran van der Sloot, 21-year-old Deepak Kalpoe, and 18-year-old Satish Kalpoe. The events that took place after that are largely contested. Through many different testimonies by witnesses and suspects, investigators would check every lead and run into heartbreaking dead ends.

Upon the morning sunrise, the graduates arrived to board the flight home. It was time to start the rest of their lives. All of the graduates arrived without problem except for one: Natalee Holloway. Through irresponsible chaperoning of a class trip and complete disregard for holding the safety of these students paramount above a fun time, an 18-year-old girl was missing. Her hotel room looked untouched from the previous evening. Her luggage safely packed in anticipation of leaving. No signs of movement in the room. Not even a towel had been disturbed. It was frighteningly clear that she had not returned to her room from the previous night's adventures. When the students and chaperones realized what was going on, they immediately notified authorities. Aruban police initiated immediate searches of the island and its surrounding waters. No trace of her was found.

Joran van der Sloot is undoubtedly the most central figure to this case. Van der Sloot was a 17-year-old Dutch honors student who lived in Aruba. At first glance, his baby face and focused eyes would seemingly make him very approachable to anyone. This was, apparently, not the first night that Natalee and Joran had met. In previous nights, they hung out at bars and engaged in behavior not known to most high school students. Over the course of the next several years, Joran would lead investigators and the Holloway family on a wild goose chase that involved changing alibis, secret videos, and fraud. The innocent appearance that Joran van der Sloot displayed was only a disguise for the true monster he would prove to be.

The Kalpoe brothers were Surinamese friends of van der Sloot. Their significance is much less publicized beyond the last sighting of Holloway. Natalee was last seen getting into Deepak Kalpoe's car with both van der Sloot and Satish. This has been confirmed true by both witnesses and suspects in one way or another. There are numerous stories told by van Sloot and other later suspects that bring the Kalpoe's back to the forefront of the case. In such a complicated investigation, Joran van der Sloot, Deepak Kalpoe, and Satish Kalpoe emerged as early suspects.

Action was fast when news reached family of the mysterious disappearance of Natalee. Her mother, Beth Twitty, immediately boarded a private jet with friends and departed for Aruba. Upon arriving in Aruba, the Twittys had started searching for themselves. They located the Holiday Inn and began asking questions. They had obtained footage from the nightclub she was last seen at. To Beth Twittys surprise, the Holiday Inn workers recognized Joran van der Sloot instantly. He had apparently been a regular in the area. The helpful Holiday Inn employees provided Beth and company with Joran's name and address. Within a mere four hours since arriving at Aruba, the Twittys had already obtained more information than investigators had been able to. The Twittys provided Aruba Police with this information. It appeared that a case was forming around Van der Sloot already. However, the mishandling of the case and poor techniques of the Aruba Police Department were already rearing their ugly head. This case would prove to be a showcase of poor work, bitter disappointment, and investigators being led around by the suspects themselves. The first lead, however, was officially created.

The Twittys and their friends went to the home of Joran van der Sloot. They were accompanied by two Aruban policemen. The fact that Van der Sloot was even allowed to be approached in this manner showed quickly the lack of thought given to the early stages of the investigation. At this early point in the case, the extent of the crime was largely unknown. Hoping for the best, the Twittys only wished to find Natalee safely at the home of Van der Sloot. Joran answered the door and initially denied even knowing who Natalee Holloway was. After being confronted with evidence of their rendezvous that morning, Van der Sloot admitted to being with Natalee. Also present at the house was Deepak Kalpoe, who was driving the vehicle that Natalee had entered in to.

Van der Sloot gave a sketchy story of what had happened after they left the nightclub. He informed the Twittys as well as the two policemen that they had taken Natalee to the California Lighthouse area. This area was near the nightclub, perhaps a few miles drive depending on the route taken. Natalee had been emphatic that she wanted to see sharks. After leaving the nightclub at 1:30 A.M. they went straight to this area to sight see. Van der Sloot informed them that they had returned Natalee to the Holiday Inn hotel where she had been staying at 2:00 A.M. Natalee, who was heavily intoxicated, stumbled exiting the vehicle. The men had offered to help Natalee to her room, however she refused their help and continued toward the entrance. It was at this time, according to Van der Sloot, that she was approached by a tall man wearing all black. Thinking this was a security guard, the men drove off. This, according to Van der Sloot, was the last interaction of any kind with Natalee Holloway that they had. Deepak Kalpoe affirmed the story and agreed with the events.

This is the initial story of the events. The initial investigation is, perhaps, the most ridiculed part in this case. Not only were the men not detained for further extensive questioning, they were completely presumed to be telling the truth. This not only wasted valuable time in finding Natalee, it also allowed suspects to plan their next move. The fact that Van der Sloot and Kalpoe had initially denied even knowing who Natalee Holloway was should have been the first sign of a problem. The second, and more major sign of a problem would come in the investigation of the hotel surveillance footage. While this was obviously looked at during the investigation, this is largely an accepted procedure that is typically done prior to confronting a potential suspect.

The surveillance footage, or lack thereof, was arguably the single biggest setback with this case. The fact that Natalee was not seen in any hotel footage that fateful morning would lend investigators to believe that Van der Sloot and Kalpoe were lying. The hitch in this was that many statements from the case could not even prove that all cameras were functional at the time. The next problem was the fact that not every entrance had a surveillance. This would leave reasonable doubt that Natalee could have been dropped off near one of these entrances that was simply inaccessible to the surveillance footage.

Investigators finally felt as though they had caught the break in the case they needed when a blood stain was found in Deepak Kalpoe's car. Searching the car that was captured on surveillance as the same one that transported Natalee Holloway from the nightclub, police discovered what appeared to be a blood stain. After lab testing and further investigation, not only was this not Natalee Holloway's blood, it could not even be proven to be blood at all. Another door was closed in the initial investigation of Natalee's disappearance.

After the first full day of investigation, United States involvement in the case began. Monetary assistance was given immediately to aid the Aruban Police Department. Additionally, American searchers sought to help with the advanced search of coastline that had been a constant since Natalee Holloway missed her flight. United States Secretary of State Condoleezza Rice stated "we are in constant contact with Aruban Police. The safe return of Natalee Holloway continues to be our priority."

Hours after missing her flight, the media's involvement in the case was tremendous. All of the major news stations in the United States began their initial coverage of the story. With little facts to go on, it was largely reported as a missing person case with no evidence of foul play. No suspects had truly been pinpointed at this point. The news of her last being seen in the early hours leaving a nightclub led several to assume the worst from the get go, however. It would not be long before Joran van der Sloot was at the fore front of the investigation as well as the ensuing media storm.

It was just six days after Holloway's disappearance that authorities made their first arrest in the case. On June 5, 2005, Abraham Jones and Nick John were placed under arrest. To this day, the exact reasoning behind their arrest is unknown. One of the men had previous encounters with the law, while both were suspected of previously pacing hotels to pick up women. Both men were security guards at a nearby hotel, the Allegro Hotel. It is likely that the statements made by Van der Sloot and Kalpoe led police to this arrest. The men were released on June 13 with no charges being placed. This is yet another example of flawed work by the investigation. It was obvious that police were trusting of Joran van der Sloot and Deepak Kalpoe from the onset. This is a largely debated topic to this day. Many wonder why Van der Sloot and Kalpoe were not arrested initially. However, this was just scratching the surface of what was to come.

On June 9, Joran van der Sloot and both Kalpoe brothers were arrested on suspicion of the kidnapping and murder of Natalee

Holloway. In hindsight, it is absolutely unfathomable that it took investigators 10 days to make these arrest. The only evidence they really had at this point was surveillance of Natalee last being seen with these men. Aruban police reported that these men were the "prime suspects from the get-go." While this may have been true to a point, police waited until June 6 to start extended surveillance of the men. Investigators knew they would need much more evidence than a video of Natalee entering a car with the men from the nightclub. Aruban Police instigated phone taps, video surveillance, tailing their vehicles, and monitoring of their e-mails. At this point, in order to continue to hold the three suspects in custody, they would need to provide increasingly substantial evidence at different check points of the investigation. With increasingly consistent pressure from Natalee Holloway's family, police decided to stop the surveillance activities prematurely and execute the arrest on the men.

The arrest of these three suspects was met with heavy interest from people all over the world. The procedures by police and the heavy involvement of the Holloway family seemingly left everyone with an opinion on what should have been conducted differently. Many media outlets focused on the timing of the surveillance activities. Having taken nearly a week to begin the activities from the time of Natalee's last sighting, many felt it was already too late to incriminate the suspects. Also, the fact that surveillance started at the time they had already arrested Adams and John was a bit odd for normal investigative procedure. Lastly, many assumed that if investigators pursued an arrest after just a few days of surveillance of the men, they must have captured something indisputable to implicate one or all of the suspects. This was simply not the case. Aruban Police had missed the initial window of the investigation. Many critics argue that in the interest of uncovering the truth, an extended surveillance would be necessary for the time period they had waited to begin. Investigators instead buckled to pressure from an unorthodox family interaction in a complicated case.

June 11 was the first of many highly publicized false leads. Aruban Minister of Justice David Cruz indicated, in a statement, that Natalee Holloway was dead and that authorities knew the exact location of her body. This was all over most any major media outlet as an early morning breaking news story. The United States was gripped with curiosity and heartbreak as it seemed the terrible truth had come to fruition. Hours later, Cruz released a follow up statement that they had been the victim of "misinformation." This simply is unacceptable. As an investigator or someone in a position as high as Cruz was, you can't put the wagon before the horse, especially to national media outlets. What was the source of this misinformation? Lead investigator Gerold Dompig reported to the Associated Press that one of the detained men had informed them that "something terrible and unthinkable" had happened on the beach after they left the nightclub. The suspect, it was reported, was leading them to the location of the body. This, of course, was another folly.

On June 16, yet another suspect, Steve Gregory Croes, was arrested. "Croes was detained based on urgent information given to us by one of the other three suspect," Aruban Police Superintendent Jan van der Straaten informed the media. While this arrest didn't yield much as far as new leads, it did start to give the appearance that investigators were at a standstill with the case. Six days later on June 22, Joran van der Sloot's father, Paulus, was arrested. This was largely believed to be a bargaining chip to use against Joran. While Paulus was not a suspect, as later revealed by police, he was interrogated in an effort to get more information on Joran. Both Croes and Paulus van der Sloot were released on June 26.

It was around this time where public opinion began to focus on Joran van der Sloot. It was quite clear to all involved that Van der Sloot was not being truthful in his story. The events made little sense to the general public. The longer that Natalee remained missing, the more likely it was that she was, indeed, dead. The suspicion on Joran would only intensify in the coming day.

From the time of the arrest of Joran van der Sloot and the Kalpoe brothers, their stories changed numerous times. In particular, Van der Sloot was giving three completely conflicting stories that would put the focus solely on him.

The first story shift came, oddly enough, from all three suspects. Van der Sloot and both Kalpoe brothers all agreed that Joran and Natalee had been dropped off at the Marriott Hotel beach near several fisherman huts. Van der Sloot was emphatic that he didn't harm Natalee Holloway in any way. He told investigators that they were both heavily intoxicated, and eventually Natalee passed out on the beach. When this happened, he began to walk home. It was at this time that he made a phone call to Deepak Kalpoe that he was walking home. Van der Sloot claims to have sent Kalpoe a text message 40 minutes later. Oddly enough, the phone call nor text message was found in Van der Sloot's phone records.

Lead investigator Gerold Dompig gave insight into the third different story by the suspects. This story, told by Joran van der Sloot, was a turning point in that it showed that he was willing to change his story however he saw fit in order to avoid suspicion.

"The latest story came when Joran saw that his buddies, the Kalpoe's, were essentially pointing the finger in his direction. He wanted to screw them by pointing the finger right back at them. But the story simply doesn't check out. He just wanted to screw Deepak. They (Deepak and Joran) had great arguments about this in front of the judge. Their stories didn't match. Joran felt the focus shifting to him and was willing to do anything to change it. That girl, she was from Alabama. She is not going to stay in the car with two black kids while Joran simply gets out of the car to head home alone. We firmly believe the second story; that they were dropped off at the Marriott. This goes along with the timeline and the stories given by the Kalpoe's."

Upon hearings in front of the judge on July 4, both Satish and Deepak Kalpoe were released from custody. Joran van der Sloot was to remain for a minimum of 60 days. Focus was solely on Van der Sloot as the main suspect in the disappearance of Natalee Holloway.

For nearly all of July, searches for Natalee Holloway remained fruitless endeavors. Investigators had no leads and were consistently getting varied stories from Joran van der Sloot. While police had solid suspicions of Van der Sloot, they had essentially zero solid evidence against him. The media storm updated the world daily on search efforts. With each passing day, reality began to set in for many that Natalee Holloway may never be found. Initially, a $50,000 reward was offered for Natalee's safe return. On July 25, the reward for the safe return of Holloway had increased all the way to $1,000,000. In addition, a $100,000 reward was offered for information that would lead to the location of her remains. In August of the same year, the reward for the location of her remains would raise all the way to $250,000. This was widely covered by the media and many local and national governments. This was a final attempt by investigators to break the cold case open. This strategy had several negative impacts, however. The most severe of these were the wasted time on false leads and folly calls. This was not anticipated by investigators as it should have been.

Between July 27 and 30, investigators initiated a massive undertaking. The pond in front of the Aruba Racquet Club was completely drained. This was within one mile of the Marriott Hotel where Van der Sloot had apparently taken Natalee Holloway. A tip was given to police that was especially unique. A gardener had apparently seen Joran van der Sloot driving into the Racquet Club with the Kalpoe brothers. Van der Sloot was said to have been hiding his face. The gardener informed police that the men were seen driving in between 2:30 A.M. and 3:00 A.M. on the morning of May 30. The search of the pond bed and surrounding area, however, yielded no clues.

On July 28, a jogger came forward with a frightening testimony. The United States media covered this story heavily for several days as it was the first story of someone seeing a woman resembling Natalee Holloway since her disappearance. The jogger claimed that she saw a group of men burying a young, blonde haired woman on the afternoon of May 30 at a landfill. The landfill was subsequently searched three separate times with precision. This search, again, yielded no results.

In late August, Joran van der Sloot became the front page villain to many. Throughout the entire case, it was well covered as to how many variations of a story Joran had given. While showing no remorse or empathy for the Holloway family, the public formed a very negative opinion of Van der Sloot. Anita van der Sloot would provide more material for the family. "It's a desperate attempt to get the boys to talk. But there is nothing to talk about. Joran has no fault in this mystery." Joran van der Sloot's mother made this statement after police again brought in the Kalpoe's for questioning. This left a bitter taste in the mouths of many. It was shaping up to be Van der Sloot's versus investigators.

On September 3, 2005, Joran van der Sloot was released from custody due to insufficient evidence to hold. By September 14, all restrictions were officially lifted from Van der Sloot. Whatever the events of May 30, no suspect was in custody and there were no leads for police. Joran van der Sloot was a free man. The release of Van der Sloot created a frenzy among the general public. People all over the United States and surrounding areas were furious, set in their beliefs that a guilty man was walking away free. The nation was gripped against a common villain.

The months that followed Joran van der Sloot's release provided media cannon fodder of epic proportions. Van der Sloot did several interviews and even composed a book of his take on the events of the night. To the public's astonishment, this man was now profiting off of this whole fire storm of a case. The most notable post release interview came with Fox News on a three night special. Van der Sloot claims that the two were heavily intoxicated on the beach after leaving the nightclub. He went into great detail about the two planning an escapade on the beach, narcotic use, and partying in a fun filled night in Aruba. He showed little empathy or remorse for any of the events. He seemingly talked about Natalee as if she was the villain. Joran went on to explain that Natalee wanted to have sex on the beach, however he didn't have a condom. He left her on the beach and was driven home by Satish Kalpoe. Later, Satish Kalpoe's lawyer claims that Satish was asleep well before this would have happened. Joran went on to explain that he was embarrassed for having left a beautiful woman alone on the beach, citing this as the reason for his ever changing story. He said that he was convinced Holloway would turn up.

This all sat so negatively to viewers. There was outrage over the handling of the investigation. People could not understand how no evidence existed to implicate a man that was deemed the perpetrator. Aruba authorities later claimed that over $3 million had been spent on the investigation. This was over 40% of the overall budget for investigative expenditures.

On December 18, 2007 after extensive efforts to implicate the Kalpoe brothers and/or Joran van der Sloot, the case was officially closed. Prosecutors cited lack of evidence to a violent crime, lack of evidence to a murder, as well as lack of continued funding for the expensive investigation. Over two full years after the disappearance of Natalee Holloway, the case was closed. The remains of Natalee Holloway had not been found. Joran van der Sloot not only was a free man, but had profited greatly from the publicity of the case. This, however, would not be the final chapter to the journey of Joran van der Sloot.

In the years after the closing of the Natalee Holloway case, Joran van der Sloot told several variations of events of that fateful morning. He gave countless interviews, seemingly telling a different story in each one of them. Ultimately, Joran van der Sloot was seeking money and fame through his disgusting actions. In an interview with Fox News in

2008, he claimed to have sold Natalee Holloway in sexual slavery. He later retracted the statements in the days after. It was reported in 2010 that in a 2009 interview with RTL group, he claimed he disposed of the body in a marsh area in Aruba. This interview was never confirmed, nor denied by investigators or Van der Sloot.

Remarkably, Van der Sloot would show his greed had no limits. On March 29, 2010 Van der Sloot contacted Beth Twittys legal representative. He offered to give the location to Natalee Holloway's remains in exchange for $25,000. After contacting police, the transaction was made. $15,000 was wired to Van der Sloot's account, and the remaining $10,000 was given by a middle man. The receipt of the transaction was videotaped by police. The information provided by Van der Sloot was proven false, as the building that he claimed housed the remains was not yet built at the time of the disappearance. Van der Sloot would be indicted on June 30 of the same year. However, he was about to be indicted for a much more serious crime.

On May 30, 2010, exactly five years from the time of the disappearance of Natalee Holloway, Stephany Flores Ramirez was reported missing in Lima, Peru. Ironically, she was found dead just three days later in a hotel room registered to Joran van der Sloot. On June 7, 2010, Van der Sloot confessed to killing Ramirez after he lost his temper while she was using his laptop. Within the same interview, he said that he knew where Holloway's body was. Dealing with jurisdiction issues, Peruvian police could not further investigate the Holloway statement without Aruban authorities.

Aruban authorities were granted interrogation of Van der Sloot in Peru in June of 2010. While he would not confess to murdering Holloway or her whereabouts, he did admit to the extortion plot on the Holloway family. "I wanted to get back at Natalee's family. They have been making my life miserable for the last five years," Van der Sloot said. Van der Sloot was found guilty in the murder of Stephany Flores

Ramirez and sentenced to 28 years in prison. This sentence also included his time for his extortion of the Holloway family.

Natalee Holloway's remains have never been found. There have never been any convictions made into the disappearance of Natalee or any criminal wrong doing. In this case, it would be naïve to imagine a scenario where Joran van der Sloot was not responsible in some way for the death of Natalee Holloway. While Van der Sloot waste the best years of his life behind bars, a young woman with an extremely bright future is still gone. Closure will never be possible for the Holloway family. Perhaps a poor investigative strategy is to blame for the lack of any convictions. Maybe it is the irresponsible planning of school personnel and behavior supervision by chaperones could have prevented this tragedy. Better decision by Natalee herself may have helped avoid such a terrible event. In any case, an intelligent young woman who had everything in front of her did not deserve this end. The Holloway family did not deserve this. We will likely never know the true events of that fateful May morning. What we do know is that we will never get to see the true potential that Natalee Holloway had.

FINDING JENNIFER: THE DISAPPEARANCE OF JENNIFER KESSE

MARY DANIELLE TAYLOR

The unsolved disappearance of Jennifer Kesse from her Orlando, Florida condo in the early hours of January 23, 2006, garnered widespread attention from the local and national media alike, leading to large-scale search parties conducted by the Orlando Police Department and FBI. However, despite the fact that Jennifer Kesse disappeared over ten years ago in the parking lot of her apartment complex, investigators are no closer to solving the case.

Jennifer Kesse, a finance manager for a Florida property and vacation company, had left her recently purchased condo in Orlando, Florida to begin her morning commute to work. However, Jennifer would never make it into work that morning, and her family and friends would never hear from her again. Read on to learn more about who Jennifer Kesse was, about the circumstances of her disappearance, and the local and national reaction to her missing persons case.

Early Life

Jennifer Kesse, a graduate of Vivian Gaither High School in Tampa, Florida, had graduated with a degree in finance from the University of Central Florida, located in Orlando, Florida, in 2003, where she also served as a member of the Alpha Delta Pi sorority. Following her graduation from college, Jennifer began working at the Central Florida Investments Timeshare Company as a finance manager.

Shortly before the date of her disappearance, Jennifer and her current boyfriend had visited Saint Croix, in the U.S. Virgin Islands, for a vacation. After returning home from the Virgin Islands by plane, Jennifer drove directly from her boyfriend's house in South Florida to her job in Ocoee, Florida for a full day of work. Jennifer would return home to her newly-purchased condo in Orlando that evening, the very same evening of her disappearance.

Night of Her Disappearance

Jennifer was last seen leaving the Westgate Resorts office of the Central Florida Investments Timeshare Company on the night of January 23, 2006 in Ocoee, Florida, after returning home from her vacation in Saint Croix, in the U.S. Virgin Islands, with her boyfriend. Several close friends and members of her family received calls from Jennifer that night, and the last call that she made before her disappearance was to her boyfriend shortly before 10:00pm.

Jennifer typically called or texted her boyfriend during her morning commute to work to wish him good morning; however, he became concerned on the morning of January 24th when he did not receive a message from her. When he attempted to call Jennifer that morning, his call was sent directly to voicemail. Because Jennifer had previously told him that she had an early-morning meeting at work, he assumed that she was busy and would call him once she received his voicemail. He continued his day at work until receiving a call from Jennifer's parents later that day informing him that she had never made it to work.

When Jennifer did not show up to work or contact her direct supervisor, a coworker contacted Jennifer's parents to express concern and see if they had heard from her. Jennifer was supposed to attend a very important work meeting with her higher-ups that morning, and it was extremely unlike her to fail to show up with calling ahead. Upon receiving the call from Jennifer's office, her parents immediately jumped into action. Her father, Drew Kesse, said "We were calling hospitals, calling jails, calling her friends, asking them to call places, calling Rob, and he tried calling her and she did not answer."

Her parents soon jumped into their car and made the two-hour drive to Jennifer's condo in Orlando, Florida from their home in Tampa. While driving, her parents contact her condo management office at *Mosaic Apartments*, located on the 3700 block Convoy Road in Orlando, and requested that the manager stop by her condo to check on her. He reported that she was not home, that her condo was in great condition, and that her car was not in the parking lot.

In addition, once her parents arrived in Orlando and entered their daughter's condo, they did not notice anything out of place or any signs of a struggle. Furthermore, they noticed that Jennifer's clothes were laid out on her bed and that a wet towel was present in the restroom, leading them to believe that Jennifer was at home that morning. Her father Drew later said, "We actually found two or three outfits laid out on her bed she was picking. Showered, shower was still damp. Her towel was still damp. Her work stuff was not there. So we knew that, OK, she got ready for work."

The parents quickly contacted the Orlando police department to report her as missing. Family members began passing out flyers that evening and reaching out to local media organizations, while the local police department began organizing a search party.

A local television reporter and friend of Jennifer's, Scott Thuman, described the family's actions like this: "I made sure they were on every TV station every single night as long as we could keep that alive. They did the networks, they did radio shows. They did every newspaper interview they could." An investigative reporter who covered the case would later say, "It was hard to go anywhere without seeing her face and her picture and also the information on her vehicle."

Timeline

<u>January 23, 2006</u>

Early Morning – Leaves her boyfriend's home in Central Florida to head directly to her office at Westgate Resorts for a full day at work. Jennifer and her boyfriend had just returned from a trip to Saint Croix, U.S. Virgin Islands.

6:00pm – Jennifer leaves her office at Westgate Resorts and drives to her condo complex in Orlando, Florida. She unpacks her clothes and contacts several family members to let them know that she has returned home from vacation safely.

10:00pm – Jennifer calls her boyfriend and speaks with him for several minutes before saying goodnight. Jennifer's boyfriend is the last known person to speak with her before her disappearance.

<u>January 24, 2006</u>

7:30am – Police believe that Jennifer was abducted sometime around 7:30am to 8:00am on the morning of the 24th. She was likely taken either while walking through the parking lot towards her car or while entering her vehicle.

8:30am – Jennifer's boyfriend calls her, but the call is sent directly to voicemail. Jennifer typically calls her boyfriend during her morning commute to say good morning and chat. He assumes that she is busy with an early-morning meeting that they had previously discussed.

11:00am – Jennifer's coworkers, concerned that she uncharacteristically did not show up to work and had missed a very important meeting, called her parents to see if Jennifer is okay. Both her parents and coworkers realize that something is wrong.

11:15am – Jennifer's parents immediately begin the two-hour drive to Jennifer's condo in Orlando from their home in Tampa. Her parents contact her condo's management office and request that they enter her condo to check on her. He reports that nothing is out of the ordinary and that her car is gone.

12:00pm – Jennifer's brother, who lives locally, arrives at her condo complex and begins looking for her. Unbeknownst to anyone at the time, a surveillance camera at an apartment complex 1 mile down the road from her own condo shows an unidentifiable man parking Jennifer's car. The video shows the suspect parking the car, and sitting in it for approximately 30 seconds before exiting the car and walking away from the complex. Unfortunately for investigators, the suspect's face was obscured by a fencing post and neither the local police department nor the FBI were able to produce a useable shot of the suspect's face.

1:00pm – Jennifer's parents arrive in Orlando and immediately enter her condo. They notice that her shower is covered with water and that her towel is still wet. They also see that her work clothes are laid out on her unmade bed, that her makeup and hairdryer are lying out on her bathroom sink, and that her pajamas are piled on the restroom floor.

Police theorize that Jennifer may have had a fight with her boyfriend and left her apartment to cool off. They preach patience to the parents.

5:00pm – Jennifer's close family and friends begin passing out missing persons flyers to local passerby. The police respond by sending a detective to her condo to gather information and investigate her disappearance. Police begin to question her family and friends, and begin to organize a search party.

<u>January 26, 2006</u>

8:10am – After seeing a report on Jennifer's disappearance on the local news, a resident at a local apartment complex calls the Orlando Police Department to report that her car has been parked in their complex for the last two days. Police arrive at the complex to verify this report, and quickly haul the car away to local police facilities for a forensic analysis. Police are finally able to identify and locate security footage showing an unidentified person parking Jennifer's car and leaving the complex by foot. This footage would lead investigators to determine that Jennifer may have been abducted.

Investigation

Jennifer's parents, as well as the initial investigators who looked into her case, noticed that Jennifer's apartment showed no signs of forced entry, her condo door was locked, and there were no signs of a struggle. Furthermore, because Jennifer's work clothes were laid out neatly and there was evidence that she had recently showered, investigators theorized that she had gotten ready for work the morning of her disappearance and had left her condo to begin her morning commute. The also assert that Jennifer likely left her apartment and was abducted either during the walk to her car or as she was entering the vehicle.

Two days after Jennifer's disappearance on January 26th, her 2004 black Chevy Malibu was located at the *Huntington on the Green* apartment complex, located at Americana Ave. and Texas, a little over a mile away from her own condo. While the apartment complex her car was parked at did have several security cameras, covering both her car and the exit to the apartment complex itself, the videos offered limited clues to her disappearance.

The video showed a "person of interest" who dropped off her car at noon the day of her disappearance; however, the best shots from the video were rendered useless since fencing from the apartment complex concealed the face of the unidentified man in three separate frames. The suspect was seen wearing an all-white uniform, leading some close to the case to believe that the suspect was a painter or other type of manual laborer.

Beau Zimmer, an investigative reporter who followed Jennifer Kesse's disappearance, described the video like this: "There's two different angles, all surrounding the pool area. But it's very, very blurry and it's hard to see. But you can see someone pulling Jennifer's car into that visitor's parking lot. They wait inside the car for a number of seconds before they get out and look around, and then walk out of frame of the picture. But the next shot of the video was what everyone thought would be so helpful. The next shot was of a person that was walking back and forth along the fence line."

However, he noted, "Every frame of the video, the person is obscured by a post and so you never see the person's face." Zimmer would later remark, "It has got to be the most frustrating thing for detectives, the most frustrating thing for the Kesse family, because for just one split second, later or earlier, you would have seen that individual's face and you would have had a better idea of what happened to Jennifer."

When investigators shared footage from the video with Jennifer's family and friends, they were unable to identify the man in question. A Fox News reporter would later say in a televised retrospective segment on the case that the obscured image made the man the "luckiest person of interest ever."

Both the FBI and NASA were called in to conduct advanced video analyses of the footage to provide more clues on the stalled case. The FBI determined that the person was roughly 5'3" to 5'5" tall, but could not offer definitive proof of the suspect's gender. Despite NASA's digital enhancement of the video, they were not able to provide any additional information that could help the case.

Despite the dead-end that the surveillance video represented, investigators were able to put together several pieces of the puzzle. Since all of Jennifer's valuables were found in her car, parked a mile down the street in a different apartment complex, they were able to determine that robbery was not a primary motive in her disappearance. In addition, a police dog was able to track a scent a full mile from her parked car back to her condo complex, leading investigators to theorize that the unidentified suspect returned to her complex directly after disposing of her car. However, police were unable to locate any helpful evidence along the route walked by the suspect.

After conducted a search and forensic analysis of her vehicle, investigators identified two pieces of evidence: a latent fingerprint from an unidentified individual and a small strand of DNA. Given the lack of evidence found in the car, coupled with the lack of clothing fibers, hair strands, and DNA, the police believe that the car was thoroughly wiped down in an attempt to remove incriminating evidence. The investigative reporter assigned to the case, Beau Zimmer, would say, "There was maybe one print and detectives think that it was maybe wiped down, and that this was an intentional act to not only hide this vehicle, but also to hide any evidence of who may have driven it."

Despite the lack of evidence found in her car, investigators did notice that several items were missing. They were unable to located her cell phone, keys, purse, clothes, briefcase, or iPod. While police are often able to track a missing person's cell phone or bank accounts for clues, her bank account was never accessed by her captors and her cell phone remained turned off with the battery removed.

Investigators quickly compiled a list of potential suspects after questioning her friends and family for clues. Her current boyfriend was questioned and quickly eliminated from the list of suspects after providing a valid alibi. In addition, Jennifer's ex-boyfriend and one of her coworkers, who had romantic feelings for Jennifer and had sought a relationship with her in the past, were interviewed by the police.

One the of the most interesting factors in Jennifer's disappearance was the fact that her condo complex was undergoing major construction at the time of her disappearance. Many of the workers, some who were undocumented immigrants, were living in the complex while it was undergoing construction. Jennifer had mentioned her discomfort with some of the workers to her family on multiple occasions, claiming that they harassed and catcalled her regularly. Jennifer's parents have also stated on multiple occasions that they believe she may have been a victim of human trafficking.

In May 2007, the CEO of Central Florida Investments Timeshare Company, David Siegel, offered a $1 million reward for information that led to her being found alive; however, the reward was never claimed. A $5,000 reward for information on her disappearance, offered by the Central Florida Crime line, remains active today.

Suspects

Ex-boyfriend

Jennifer had recently broken up with a previous boyfriend, and he was reportedly very angry about the breakup and the fact that Jennifer was now dating another man. Beau Zimmer would report that Jennifer's ex-boyfriend became incredibly angry after finding out that she was travelling to Saint Croix with Rob, saying "The night before or sometime before, he had been out drinking and gotten drunk and apparently he was upset that he was not the one that was with Jennifer.

Zimmer would later remark that the ex-boyfriend was cleared by the police, saying "They talked with him several times, and while police say he is not a suspect in the case, certainly you get the feeling from others that he should be talked to a little bit more."

Current Boyfriend

Jennifer's boyfriend, Rob, was initially considered a suspect in her disappearance. The couple had just returned from a vacation in Saint Croix, in the U.S. Virgin Islands, and Rob was the last person who had spoken with Jennifer the night before her disappearance. Police soon interviewed Rob to learn more about his relationship with Jennifer and to ascertain his whereabouts the morning of her disappearance.

However, Rob was quickly discounted as a suspected. Rob had an airtight alibi; he was more than 200 miles away when Jennifer was abducted, at his home in Fort Lauderdale, Florida. Investigative journalist Beau Zimmer says, "The police said that between his phone records and the fact that he was in South Florida, we don't believe that he was involved."

The police department's belief in Rob's innocence is shared by Jennifer's family. He was fully cooperative with the police department and FBI's investigation and willingly provided a DNA sample twice. Jennifer's father, Drew Kesse, said "Rob has been put over the coals, Rob has been polygraphed three of four times, Rob has been interviewed probably over a dozen times."

Coworker

Both Jennifer's family, friends, and coworkers reported that Jennifer had recently turned down a coworker who was hitting on her and attempting to strike up a romantic relationship. Jennifer's mom, Joyce, said that the coworker was married and was refusing to accept Jennifer's decision not to date him, both because he was married and because she did not date people she worked with. Joyce later said, "Jennifer arranged to meet him in the cafeteria at work so that once and for all she could tell him, 'Leave me alone, I am never going to date you. And besides, I don't date married men.'"

The police department did question Jennifer's coworker and eventually eliminated him from the list of suspects. However, Joyce said "We feel it should have been consistent to keep the pressure on that individual."

Construction Workers

Jennifer, who had just purchased and moved into her newly renovated condo two months before her disappearance, had repeatedly expressed concern about construction workers in her complex. The complex, which was undergoing extensive renovations at the time, was housing undocumented immigrants working on the consecution projects, at the time of her disappearance. Beau Zimmer has stated, "Jennifer told some of her friends that she felt really uncomfortable around some of these guys. Apparently there may have been some cat calls and things like that."

Jennifer's parents have also stated that she may have been abducted by a construction worker, with her mother saying, "I can't help wonder if someone was stalking her from afar that she didn't even know. Could there have been someone watching her comings and goings?"

The local police department did question many of the construction workers who were working at her condo complex at the time of her disappearance; however, no leads would develop from this line of questioning. Zimmer would say, "The police tried to talk to as many of the workers that would have been there when Jennifer disappeared, but they acknowledge that they may have missed some people."

Sex Traffickers

Drew Kesse has claimed that it is well-known that there was an active sex trafficking ring in the Orlando area at the time of Jennifer's disappearance, which her parents think may be linked to her abduction. Jennifer's father, Drew Kesse, has stated "My gut feeling to this day, honestly, I truly believe she was trafficked." His sentiment was echoed by Jennifer's close friend and local television reporter Scott Thuman, was said "It would make sense on a lot of levels, as unfortunate as it is."

Reaction

The disappearance of Jennifer Kesse led to nationwide outrage and attention, with coverage in the local, state, national, and international media. At the behest of Orlando Police Department chief Val Demings, the FBI took over control of the case on June 10, 2010 and remains in-charge of her missing persons case to this day. She remains on the FBI's Missing List and they continue to search for her and react to current leads, with the most recent search taking place in February 2014. She is also still considered still missing by the Orlando Police Department, Interpol, and the Orange County, Florida Police Department.

In reaction to Jennifer's disappearance and the investigation into her disappearance. The Florida House of Representatives passed Senate Bill 502, entitled "The Jennifer Kesse and Tiffany Sessions Missing Persons Act," by unanimous vote on May 2, 2008. This bill changed the way that missing persons cases are handled in the state of Florida, instituting reforms such as allowing the Florida Department of Law Enforcement to provide assistance in missing persons cases involving adults. Prior to the passage of this law, the FDLE was limited in its ability to provide assistance in cases involving the disappearance or abduction of adults aged 26 or older.

THE DISAPPEARANCE OF TARA CALICO

NICK PESCI

<u>Tara Calico Mystery</u>

The story of Tara Calico is one of confusion, uncertainty, and sadness. The events of her disappearance are one of the least understood of any crime over the past 50 years. A single Polaroid showing what is widely believed to be Tara, ultimately gives her disappearance its most notable name: The Polaroid Mystery.

Tara Calico was born on February 28, 1969 to loving parents in New Mexico. She led the typical American childhood. She had a huge amount of friends and extended family. Many were drawn to her bright personality and contagious smile. Even at an early age, she was developing into a tall, athletic young woman. She took a great interest in sports and outdoor activities. Among her favorite things to do was biking, hiking, and camping.

Tara Calico succeeded greatly in school. She had a strong interest in most every subject. Her parents would describe her as "the sweetest girl who never wanted to get in trouble". She had earned an opportunity to continue her education at the University of New Mexico at Valencia.

She had also formed a strong relationship with her boyfriend around the time she turned 18 years old. The two were seemingly a perfect match. Instead of movies and dinners, this couple preferred biking and walking, most any activity that required physical activity. Tara's parents enjoyed seeing her so happy. When she was just 19 years old, however, things would change forever.

On the morning of September 20, 1988 everything would change for Tara and her family. She was in a joyful mood. She was enjoying a day off from school at her family home in Belen, New Mexico. The weather was perfect. It was a mild morning and a great climate to get out and enjoy the day. Tara was an avid biker. She decided to embark on a long, 17 mile bike route that would ultimately lead to her returning back to her home in Belen.

She planned to leave at 9:30 A.M. The route she would take would make an elaborate oval that would take her around the railroad tracks as well as the Rio Communities Golf Course. The route had some definite scenic areas, especially the trail along the railroad tracks. The beautiful weather meant that she would be able to make great time on the trip.

She had a lunch date with her boyfriend for noon. The couple planned to play tennis that afternoon. She had made a phone call to her boyfriend that morning and everything was completely normal. Looking back at the entire event, there was one thing that eerily stood out to her family. Before Tara left for her bike ride, she had told her mother jokingly that "if she wasn't back by noon, to come look for her." This was meant to be a playful banter between Tara and her mother, but ultimately could not have been any truer. This was the ultimate, real life foreshadowing that would turn out to be such a nightmare for all involved. Upon leaving for her bike ride at 9:30 A.M. she made her statement and rode off into the gorgeous morning air. This would be the last time anyone would see her alive in person.

Noon approached, and passed. Tara's mother became a bit anxious at the whole situation. Specifically, Tara was not one to arrive late or not show up when she was supposed to. All her mother could think of was the grim last words she had been told by Tara. As 12:30 P.M. approached, Patty Doel, Tara's mother, decided to look along the route she had taken to quell her worries. At this point, Patty felt it was likely that Tara was just running behind or maybe even stopped to enjoy the beautiful day. All that being said, Patty got in her car and went out to search along the route.

Patty got in her car and headed south on N.M. 47. This led to the Rio Communities where she would spend the majority of her trek. Seeing no sign of Tara in the least, full panic began to set in for Patty. Perhaps she had taken an alternate route or had merely stopped to see a friend. As it approached 1:00 P.M. Patty knew something was wrong. A strong sense of uneasiness came over Patty Doel. Something just wasn't right. By this time, she had missed her tennis date with her boyfriend and was entirely too late to assume that she had just been riding at a slow pace.

Tara was a teenager who rode her bike religiously. A 17 mile ride would not take near this long, especially with a known route that she had used many times before. Something was terribly wrong, and it was up to Patty to figure out what that may be.

Patty continued to circle the roads around the Rio Communities. She decided it may be best to creep along the shoulder of the road in an attempt to see into the ditches. Maybe Tara had an accident and was stuck in the ditch. What Patty would find would confirm her worst fear.

Patty Doel froze as she saw something laying on the side of the road. It was a Boston cassette tape.

Tara Calico was a typical teenage girl for the time as she loved music. She was a huge fan of Boston. Most any bike ride that Tara would take would feature a water bottle, helmet, and her Sony Walkman. Most often, she would be listening to Boston.

The morning of September 20 was no different. She had her water bottle, helmet, and her Sony Walkman. She had a Boston cassette tape to accompany her on her long bike ride that morning.

As Patty approached the cassette tape and noticed that it was Boston, she lost all control of her worries. She knew in her heart that something was terribly wrong. Patty Doel immediately called police.

An expansive search of the area followed. Police questioned her family to get a sense of any possible place she could have went. Investigators initially believed that she was likely at a friend's house and failed to notify her mother. After all, she was a 19 year old college student. She easily could have felt that it was not necessary to notify her mother of minor changes to her day like this. Patty knew better. Patty suspected foul play. She also felt that Tara was smart enough to have left the Boston cassette as a clue to investigators and her mother that something wasn't right.

All those that were interviewed agreed that Tara was not the kind to vanish without notifying those around her. She had never done anything like that before, and she had no reason to have done it then. Her boyfriend agreed, citing that she had never missed a date they had scheduled and would never "stand him up", especially for an activity such as tennis or anything else physical. At this point, full panic mode had been reached by everyone who was at all close to Tara. It was now a race against the clock.

At this point, police were quite skeptical of the entire situation. A Boston cassette on the side of the road and a 19 year old woman who was late returning home was, in their mind, just simply not enough to conduct a full missing person report. After all, there were thousands of Boston cassette, presumably, in the area. If a missing person report and search was filed each time a 19 year old was late coming home, then there would be hundreds of such reports each day.

Everything changed for police later that day. A policeman spotted a pink Huffy bicycle in a ditch along with a Sony Walkman roughly 20 miles from the home of Tara Calico. This changed everything. Police were now as convinced as Tara's family that something substantial had happened to her. Her bicycle, Walkman, and Boston cassette found thrown in the ditch caught their attention. Moreover, the location of the bicycle being so far from the home alerted police that she had either been taken from this location, or perhaps had been taken closer to her home and the bike and Walkman were simply thrown out at this point. Either way, investigators knew they had a major problem on their hands. They also knew that time was of utter importance if there was any hope to find Tara alive. They would need to work fast and efficiently.

New Mexico detectives began to put all of their resources to this case. They questioned anyone around the seen and interviewed hundreds of people. Being as the route that Tara was to take was so long, they felt confident that someone, somewhere saw something of importance that may lead to a break in the case. Several people confirmed that a 1953 Ford F-150 pickup truck had been seen following Tara just a few miles from her house. This truck had an attached camper shell on it, which would prove significant. It was not known if Tara Calico knew who these people were, or even if she was aware someone was behind her. After all, she had music blaring in her ears from her Walkman which likely would have made it impossible for her to hear anything behind her.

Investigators felt it was significant to understand a bit about the social aspect of Tara. Tara Calico was a tall, athletic young woman who anyone would say was an attractive woman. There were many men who wanted to be with her and date her, and she was vocal to her friends about how she was approached many times by men asking her out. Her boyfriend affirmed this, as he said men had even approached her when they were together. Investigators thought this was significant for two reasons. First, Tara may very well have known who these people were. If she knew who was in the F-150, she may have simply been ignoring them and continuing on her route. Second, Tara may not have understood the present danger by strangers approaching her. After all, she had been approached on numerous occasions by strangers and may have just chalked it up to another guy trying to get a date with her. All in all, police could neither prove nor support these theories without more evidence. Finding a motive or a reason in an effort to gain a lead would prove near impossible.

Even with extensive investigation by New Mexico police, the case really had no lead. The 1953 Ford F-150 was searched for in the area. However, it was not found. Tara Calico was proven to be on the bike trails and the streets around the trails on her 17 mile route. It was also confirmed that her bike and Sony Walkman were those that were found by police on the day of her disappearance. With eye witness testimony and her last known activity before her disappearance, police had nothing at all to work on for the case. She had seemingly disappeared without a trace beyond her bike and Walkman. The case ran cold for almost a year. Posters were put out, local news showed her picture and garnered attention to a hotline number for information on whereabouts. Family members urged anyone who knew anything suspicious to come forward. Rewards were offered by police and family members alike. There just weren't any leads in the case. Life would drag along for the family of Tara and her boyfriend, who was actually a suspect early in the case as police searched for answers. The whole situation was a sad reminder that closure may not come in this case, and that Tara may never be found alive. What started as a beautiful day that was perfect for a bike ride, turned into the worst nightmare for all of those involved. Police, however, finally caught a break in the most unlikely of cases. What would be discovered would be the single piece of evidence that would put this case on a national stage, and would ultimately give the case its name.

As the months dragged on, few within the family of Tara Calico thought any answers would arrive. In June of 1989, a break in the case would come. The harsh reality of this break, however, was that it would bring about many more questions with fewer answers.

It was a blistering summer for most all of the United States. In Port St. Joe, Florida, the heat was at an extreme. In this unlikely place, the name of Tara Calico would be brought to the forefront.

Port St. Joe Florida is just over 1,600 miles away from Belen, New Mexico. The story of Tara Calico had been scarcely seen in this distant place. On a June afternoon, nearly 9 full months since Tara Calico disappeared from Belen, New Mexico, a woman came upon something on the ground in a grocery store parking lot that caught her eye. As she walked closer to the strange object laying on the ground, she discovered it to be a single Polaroid photograph. This obviously peaked her curiosity. She decided that she would pick this photograph up. The striking image she would discover would open the case of Tara Calico up in a way never imagined.

The photograph showed a grave image. There were two people in the photograph. One of the people was a teenage woman, the other, a young boy, perhaps around ten years old. Both of them had black tape covering their mouths, not wrapped all the way around the head but just about ear to ear across the mouth. Each of them had their hands seemingly tied behind their backs, although the hands are out of picture so any further information on this is solely based on assumption. The woman is tall, having very long legs and a slight discoloration on the right calf, appearing to be a scar of some sort. She is wearing black gym style shorts with a grey t-shirt. She has dark colored hair that is pulled back behind her head. Nearly her whole body is visible in the photograph. The boy is in the background angle of the photograph. He is much younger than the female in the picture, and he too has black tape over his mouth in the same manner. His hands are also behind his back, assumed to be tied up. He is wearing a light blue t-shirt.

The face of each of them tell a story. The look of fear is much more present on the young boys face. They look tired and confused and are both staring directly at the camera.

The photo appears to have been taken in the back of a van of some sort. Both of the apprehended people are on blankets and pillows lying down with their heads against the side of the structure. The background is dark, creating an image that appears to have no light directly in their area, rather light that is coming in from the front of the structure behind the person taking the photograph.

In the bottom left corner of the photograph is a book. The book titled *My Sweet Andria* was written by V.C. Andrews. This would prove to be a key clue to investigators.

The woman quickly turned in the photograph to authorities. Upon investigation of the area, witnesses reported that a white Toyota cargo van had been parked in the area that morning. The van nor the driver were ever located. Witnesses described the driver of the van to be in his 30's with a thick handlebar style mustache. He was reported to be slender and of extremely fair complexion. He would never be located officially by investigators.

Investigators quickly noticed a striking resemblance to Tara Calico. Patty Doel was brought in to study the photograph and was convinced that it was Tara. Upon close review and a bit of background on Tara, she had strong reason to believe so.

The woman in the Polaroid was tall, athletic, and very slender toned. This matched Tara exactly. The hair color matched as well as the facial features and shape. The scar on the right leg of the woman in the photograph was also a chilling resemblance to one that Tara had. These clues in themselves were enough to safely attest that the girl in the photograph was, in fact, Tara Calico.

In addition to the physical features of the woman in the photograph was the odd placement of the book next to her. The book was written by V.C. Andrews, which was oddly enough the favorite author of Tara. She had read all of the V.C. Andrews books and was an avid reader. This, to many investigators and to Patty Doel, was the final piece of evidence to prove that the woman in the photograph was Tara Calico. But who was the boy in the photograph?

The young boy in the Polaroid appeared to be between 9 and 11 years old. Investigators initially believed the young boy to be Michael Henley. Michael went missing in April of 1988 in Zunis Mountain, New Mexico. He was camping with his family when he wandered off and never returned to the campsite. This would make the most sense to investigators as is would explain why Tara Calico was in the photograph as well. Both of the victims would have been assumed to have been taken from the same area around the same time.

In 1990, however, Michael Henley's remains were found just a few miles from the area that the family had been camping. It was determined that he died from exposure to the elements after presumably becoming lost in the wilderness of the area and not being able to find his way back. This was a turning point in the case as it raised doubts in the investigators minds as to the true identity of the people in the photograph.

Another problem that investigators had with the photograph was the legitimacy of the photo itself. Several people claimed that the Polaroid appeared staged. While this is a grim thought that is a terrible thing to assume, it was in fact a reality of the times. Singer Marilyn Manson famously set photos similar to this out randomly in this area as a prank. Most investigators, however, felt this photo was legitimate and not in any way staged.

Joel Nugent believed the photo to be entirely genuine. Joel Nugent was the lead investigator of the Florida case as a part of the Gulf County Sheriff's Department.

"It obviously is two kids with terror written all over them. It's kind of a bad time when you have to look at something like that and wonder. No one knows for sure if the picture was a setup. Some people think it was a stage photograph, but it was a real look of fear for me."

On September 20, 1989 *Unsolved Mysteries* aired a special on the Tara Calico disappearance. It marked the one year anniversary of her disappearance. Months prior, in July 1989, a special on Tara was aired on *A Current Affair.* Additionally, as the months turned into years, and the years turned in to decades, the story of Tara Calico was shown to a National audience on several other venues including *48 hours* and *America's Most Wanted.* With all of the exposure came an influx of tips and leads for investigators to sort through. The case of the disappearance of Tara Calico remained unsolved with no credible leads. The investigation was entirely cold.

It was not until 2008, nearly 20 years since Tara had disappeared, that this case would return to the fore front of the media. Valencia County, New Mexico Sheriff Renee Rivera released a statement claiming that he knew exactly what had happened to Tara. The problem, however, that he indicated is that the body of Tara Calico had never been found. This would make it impossible to bring those responsible, or at least who he felt was responsible, to justice.

"The individuals who did harm to Tara knew who she was. They knew who she was, and they are all local individuals. And I believe that the parents of the attackers were some of the people that helped the individuals with hiding the truth or hiding the body or trying to escape persecution," Rivera said.

Rivera never gave the suspects names. Rivera did, however, give his belief on what happened to Tara. Sheriff Rivera claims that two teenagers, roughly the same age as Tara, were involved in the crime. He also believed that several of the men's family members helped to cover up the crime.

"You know it's very frustrating, being that there's a lot of people who know what happened," Rivera said. "They know the whereabouts of the body or the remains. I believe that the body is somewhere very close. The body is somewhere very nearby."

Rivera had been approached by many informants over the previous couple of years. The informants all shared similar stories to what really happened to Tara Calico. According to the informants and Renee Rivera's statements, Tara never made it more than a few miles from her house on September 20, 1989. She was struck by the two teenagers who were driving a pickup truck. Rather than alert authorities and handle the situation the right way, the boys told their families and the families helped to bury the body of Tara Calico. The informants attest that the intention was not to hit Tara Calico, but to approach her while she was on her bike.

"She was really pretty young girl. She was very athletic, and a lot of guys wanted to talk to her, they wanted to meet her, they wanted to go out with her. And while she was riding her bike, they went up to try to talk to her, try to grab her, whatever, while she was on the bike," Rivera said.

Many people have questioned the basis of Sheriff Rivera's claims. While the claims do make sense and would line up with the evidence that investigators had uncovered, why is it 20 years later that the Sheriff would come out and voice these claims. If Rivera had such strong reason to make these allegations and had informants that were willing to speak as to what happened, why has there been no conviction? This is a question that remains to be answered.

Sadly, in 2006, Patty Doel, the mother of Tara Calico, passed away. She dealt with such a heavy heart and severe burden since Tara's disappearance in 1989. She passed away never knowing the truth as to what happened to Tara on the fateful day. Tara's father passed away in 2002 as well. Tara Calico's family never recovered from that dreadful morning, and never got the answers they needed for any sort of effort of closure. Tara's family is still searching for the truth of the events of that day. Thanks to social media, there are thousands of people nationwide that have joined in to find any answers or leads that may result in the truth.

The identity of the boy in the photograph still remains a mystery as well. The fact that neither victim in the photograph has ever been fully confirmed or identified remains a great mystery. While most every investigator will attest that woman in the photograph is indeed Tara Calico, there is no way to match an identity without the actual DNA evidence.

The story of Tara Calico is undeniably tragic. The truth is largely unknown. There have been no arrest and no attempts at arrest in the years since the horrific disappearance. While many believe the overall story that Sheriff Rivera told as to what had really happened to Tara, there has been no attempts to convict anyone of the heinous crime. The only true fact of this case is that a promising future was cut short while she was enjoying a beautiful September day. Perhaps one day the mystery of Tara Calico will be fully understood. Perhaps one day justice will come forth and healing can begin.